STUDENTSCAPE

DISCOVERING THE NEW LANDSCAPE OF UNIVERSITY

ISBN 978-0-955927713

Cover and Layout Design by James Norton
www.greenflashmedia.co.uk

First published in 2008, reprinted in 2011 & 2013 by Fusion UK

Fusion UK is a company limited by guarantee registered in England and Wales No. 3679369 and
registered charity No. 1073572.

Fusion UK, Unit 18, The Office Village, North Road, Loughborough, LE11 1QJ.
www.fusion.uk.com | 01509 268 505 | hello@fusion.uk.com

STUDENTSCAPE

DISCOVERING THE NEW LANDSCAPE OF UNIVERSITY

Table of Contents

Preparing for Studentscape

DISCOVERING THE NEW LANDSCAPE OF UNIVERSITY

Welcome

Life with God is an adventure. Adventures are journeys of discovery: we can discover more about God more about ourselves and more about the world around us. For many the university years are a defining part of that adventure and this resource is designed to prepare you for the full experience of studentscape The new landscape of university awaits and it is best to start the adventure prepared.

Over the last 12 years I've advised over 200 churches on student ministry and been part of a local church community that has welcomed over 700 students from every church background and none. We hav actively sought to serve and encourage students to live for God, love their friends and get the most out of their time at university. This resource distils some of that experience and knowledge so that you can b fully prepared for studentscape.

Go for it!

Rich

About the author
Rich Wilson

Rich is the National Team Leader for Fusion. He is responsible for building partnerships with students, churches and other organisations. Rich is married to Ness and has lived in Loughborough since studying there as a student. He has been involved in the leadership of Open Heaven Church alongside Ness since graduating from university in 1995.

Who is studentscape for?

Studentscape has been written with the 18-25 age group in mind and is a values-based approach to discipleship. It has been specifically written for those in or going into higher and further education and is an essential resource for every young person who intends on going to college or university.

How to use studentscape

Studentscape looks at a different topic for each month. The resource can be studied each month in the year leading up to university, as a crash course over the summer or during university.

It can be worked through with a friend, with a youth leader/mentor, in a small group or even on your own. Each month's content is written in such a way as to allow students to talk through the challenges together and also reflect personally on what they mean for them. The principles and values that are looked at over these months are mirrored at university and in life.

It is recommended that everyone has their own copy for completing the exercises and for future reference once at university. Here's how we recommend you use this resource in different settings.

With a friend

Not only will this prepare you for university it will deepen your friendships. Be as honest and as vulnerable as you dare and you will get loads out of it.

With a youth leader/mentor

If you don't have one, try asking someone whom you respect who can walk this journey of preparation with you.

In a small group

This could be a cell group or a specific group that comes together to get to grips with preparing for university.

On your own

Going through this resource on your own is better than not going through it at all. God will speak to you and prepare you and bring people into your life to work through the things you can't do on your own.

Themes and Tools

Each month there is a different travelling companion (a character from the Bible) to learn from and explore the landscape with, and some common themes and tools to aid your journey of discovery.

Themes

Themes are metaphors for the everyday things that make up your journey through studentscape.

LANDSCAPE

The landscape represents the topic to be discussed that month. It gives an overview and backdrop to the subject to be explored in that particular chapter.

TRAVELLING COMPANION

This is a biblical buddy, a person from the Bible, whom we can learn from and who will help apply God's truth into our everyday lives.

MOUNTAINS

Mountains represent the challenges and obstacles we face. They can be in our past, present or future. We must find ways of overcoming them.

LAKES

These are the deep waters of truth. As we turn to scripture for help and inspiration they can also become internal reservoirs to draw on as we understand and apply the different biblical passages.

STREAMS

Streams represent the continual flow of water necessary for sustaining life. The apostle Paul urges us to pray continually and be spiritually sustained by bringing things to God in prayer.

Tools

Tools are metaphors for the everyday resources that can help you on your journey through studentscape.

CAMPFIRE

Around the campfire is our community, our friendship group. It is a place of fellowship and fun and where we plan and talk through what it is we need to do together.

TENT

A one man tent creates an environment for making decisions to take personal responsibility. Godly habits and disciplines that need to be cultivated and things that must be done alone can be considered in the tent.

COMPASS

A regular glance at the compass will ensure we travel in the right direction. We need to be looking to God regularly to affirm our chosen path and stay close to his ways.

ROPE

Rope enables us to overcome difficult terrain and tackle the ups and downs in life. It represents the resources, relationships and wisdom that can help us conquer the mountains and other challenges.

Landscape: Destiny

TAKING HOLD OF YOUR FUTURE

If studentscape is on the horizon or the new day of university life has already broken then it is time to mix your plans in with God's agenda. This is the recipe for taking hold of our future in God and shining a bit more light on our destiny!

Nelson's shoes

Deep in the township of Soweto lies a modest dwelling amongst the other shanty shacks and squalor. Inside, this is a place of significance. In the corner of the bedroom sits a table with two pairs of shoes lying on it. To the sharp eye and enquiring mind there is something odd about one pair of these simple black shoes. The soles are worn oddly. They are the shoes worn in solitary confinement by Nelson Mandela towards the end of his 27-year sentence on Robben Island.

A few years ago a specialist in forensic science was granted permission to take the shoes from Mandela's old home and carry out tests on them. The tests revealed that a man had run consistently and quite vigorously for hours on end probably in one place. The implications provoked interest and eventually the question was put to Mandela himself.

Mandela confirmed it was true - he had run each day. After a day's hard labour, only one visitor a year for 30 minutes and only being allowed to send or receive a letter every six months Mandela was a seemingly helpless prisoner confined to his cell. But Mandela ran with hope in his heart. He said, simply, he had worked out his destiny. He needed to stay fit because one day, as an old man, he would be called to lead his country. From Prisoner to President!

> *'Those who dream by night in the dusty recesses of their minds wake in the day to find that all was vanity; but the dreamers of the day are dangerous men, for they may act their dream with open eyes, and make it possible.'*

(T. E. Lawrence, Lawrence of Arabia)

Travelling companion

Our travelling companion for this first month is Joseph. A dreamer by nature and gifted by God, Joseph boldly shared his first dreams with his brothers, prophesying that they would all bow down to him in the future. What started as a dream was formed into a destiny.

Lakes
Read Genesis 37:1-20

Tent

We are going to learn how to dream with God. Take a few moments in a quiet place on your own and consider:

What comes naturally to you? Think about how you deal with people. Are you persuasive, a good listener, do you have clarity of mind when analysing situations? Do you have academic, creative, musical or sporting abilities? What are you passionate about? Write your thoughts in the box below.

Wisdom Box

You've just highlighted areas of God's gifting within you. Can you identify any hopes, dreams and aspirations where you hope to use your gifting?

1.For your 3-5 years at University?

_____

2.Is there a career or vocation you'd like to fulfil?

_____

3.When you reach the end of your journey how would you like to be remembered?

_____

We can learn from Joseph that we need to be careful how, when and with whom we share our dreams.

Mountains

God loves that we have dreams and ambitions in our lives. He wants us to have life to the full by living to honour and please him. Accomplishing great feats for God is an amazing privilege, although we need to be careful that life's mountains don't end up sidetracking or blocking our destiny – the enemy wants to stop us! In order to combat this we need to be involving God in our decisions and be submitted to his lordship. We also need to understand the culture around us, which we're immersed in and are a part of.

Our generation (those born in 1981 or after) has been labelled 'Generation Y' or 'Millennials' by sociologists. We live life with the lens of 'How do I look?' in our minds. The media often target our appearance and are full of empty promises that tempt our desire for the quick fix. Our culture expects instant results.

One challenge facing many young adults is society's belief that sex outside a committed marital relationship will satisfy the needs for intimacy and love. Other cultural trends are that binge drinking, or social drug taking offer a pathway to feeling free and being yourself. Careers advice is often based on the premise that a certain amount of wealth will result in security, comfort and fulfilment. All of these and more can stifle our destiny and lead us away from God's best.

What are some of the things that you face that can steal your destiny away from you?

1. _____

2. _____

3. _____

Lakes
Read Genesis 39-41

Joseph the dreamer could hardly have suspected the tortuous dance his dream would lead him. 'And we shall see what shall become of his dreams' - there is irony in these last words of the brothers. They were determined that Joseph's dream would come to nothing and so leave their world unchallenged and untouched. But their very actions against him became the impetus that set in motion that long journey which took Joseph to Egypt and to power; power which, years later, put him in a position to supply food and shelter to his family now in desperate need.

On the way Joseph faced the rejection of his family, a faked death, a horrible pit, a slave auction, refugee status in Egypt, poverty, false accusation, sexual harassment, prison, the threat of execution and years of hard labour. All this lay between the dream and its fulfilment. And only in the treading out of that journey did the vision prove its power.

Campfire
How did Joseph keep his integrity on the way to fulfilling his dreams?

Rope
Here are 3 keys we can learn from Joseph to fulfilling destiny:

Key 1: '50:20' Vision

'God turned into good what you meant for evil'

(Genesis 50:20)

The author Rob Parsons uses this term as it encapsulates Joseph's mindset in Genesis 50:20. Initially Joseph was bold and even arrogant as he 'promptly' told his brothers of his dreams (Genesis 37: 5-11). The result was that they sold him into slavery and Joseph endured much hardship. Joseph's mind remained innocent and God-focussed. The '50:20' vision enabled him to see that after being hurt, there was still an all powerful God, who desired to partner with him in changing the world (read Romans 8:28). In Genesis 50:20 we see Joseph reflect on his earlier prediction humbly acknowledging God's plans and purposes.

Campfire
So, what does 50:20 vision mean for you?

Key 2: Character Formation
Joseph demonstrated that destiny is as much about how we embrace the whole journey as about reaching the destination. Who we are becoming is the primary destination of our destiny! Our character being formed along the way into the image of Christ is what matters most to God. It is the foundation upon which our gifts are to be built. Scripture infers that it is often our response to the fiercest trials that can shape our character the most and get us ready for responsibility.

9

Tent

Hard times can be the robbers of hopes and dreams, but God wants to use them as the impetus for healing, dependence on him and the doorway to destiny. Take some time to think how you respond to hard times and whether you are open to God teaching you and forming you in those times.

Streams

Spend some time praying with a friend, inviting God into these things and also for courage and boldness to overcome past and present mountains.

Key 3: Just Do It

Some people wait months or even years to do something about a dream. Others sadly spend a lifetime preparing for it to happen, but the fact is that they are putting it off. Dr Anthony Campolo talks of a sociological study in which fifty people over the age of ninety-five were asked one question: 'If you could live your life over again, what would you do differently?' The open-ended question was met with a multiplicity of answers from the respondents. However, three answers emerged to dominate the results of the study:

1. If I had it to do over again, I would reflect more.
2. If I had it to do over again, I would risk more.
3. If I had it to do over again, I would do more things that would live on after I am dead.

John Wimber famously spelt faith as R-I-S-K. The thing about risk is that we can end up looking at it through the lens of success or failure and never play a hand, which is ultimately the biggest loss.

'Success is never final. Failure is never fatal. It's courage that counts.'

(Winston Churchill)

Joseph had a 'just do it' attitude and even though he made a few mistakes he believed the dream that God had given to him and courageously pursued it.

Campfire

Preparation for university life is underway and great opportunities are ahead. Discuss together what the things are, real or imaginary, that stop you from doing things for God or other people? How can you start to overcome them today?

'Expect great things of God. Attempt great things for God'

(William Carey)

What is God saying to you?

Wisdom Box

10

Prayer

Father God, thank you that you promise life to the full and that my destiny is in your hands, and yet also dependant on my choices. Help me to become all that you intended by responding well to life's challenges. I pray that my dreams will reflect your dreams. Amen.

Landscape: Work

Starting in work – Works in progress – A life's work

These are all expressions used to describe something that occupies the majority of our waking hours during a lifetime. Work brings people together and many relationships are built through and around it. The lead up to university demands particular hard work in the form of study, but it is important we understand the values and principles behind our work.

Work can be about using our talents or just a means to an end. For some it is about survival and for others about leaving a legacy. Whether it's a child persevering with French verbs, a home-worker preparing meals for the children, a project manager on a building site or a missionary immersing themselves in a different culture, our exertions are the opportunity we have to leave something of significance.

Striving to keep standing

The average Briton works 48 hours per week, more than any other nation in Europe. Due to technological advances, productivity has doubled in the last 20 years! However, with employers pushing hard in order to keep pace with the competition we are now working longer than ever before.

Law firms in London have even built bedrooms into their offices for those late nights and early mornings and some employees believe that saying no may endanger their job prospects. A fear culture presides.

Paradoxically, many radio stations pump out the message of 'We're here to help you get through this'… Seemingly, for many, all they do is work and yet plodding through the drudgery often appears the goal itself.

Write down 5 words you associate with work:

1. _____

2. _____

3. _____

4. _____

5. _____

Christians aren't immune to misconceptions surrounding work and it is important we take our view of work from God – the ultimate inventor and the original worker!

Lakes
Read Genesis 1:1-25

God is a worker:

'In the beginning God created…'

(Genesis 1:1 NIV)

The first verb in the Bible (bara - created) shows God at work and also shows work is a purposeful activity that did not begin by human initiation but by God. God works and then God rests and the result is satisfaction. God rests, not because He is weary, but because He has completed what He set out to do.

Travelling companion
Adam, the first human worker is journeying along with us this month. From the Genesis account we hope to discover some of God's original plan and purpose through work.

Lakes
Read Genesis 1:26-31

God is into image:

'God patterned them after himself'

(Genesis 1:27)

God does not suffer from low self-esteem or a negative self-image. His image and everything made in that image is sacred. Our origin is in God and so it is really, really good. Original goodness came before original sin. God invested the very best of Himself into us, therefore we are highly valued in His sight and He is highly committed to us.

Through bearing the image of God and being made like Him, humanity receives an incredible significance. Our worth comes before our work and we cannot earn our worth through work.

Campfire
Discuss the things that you may do in an attempt to gain self worth. Write them down below. Think about where you may do them and who you may do them for.

Wisdom Box

13

Work because we are worth it

As humans we receive the image of God (1:26) and then the blessing of work (1:28). Our worth comes first and our work should follow. We do not work to gain self-worth; we work as a result of our self-worth.

Adam was given significance and purpose through his work in the Garden of Eden. Adam had two main jobs in Eden. The first was defined by the Hebrew word Abad which means 'to tend' – it was to use his God-given gardening skills to design, order, master and develop Eden. The second, Shamar was 'to protect' it – to prevent the devil from getting in, guarding what was good (which is where Adam was off having an unnecessary tea break…)

Mountains

- Work can be boring – it can be hard toil and sometimes drudgery.
- Motivation can be a struggle for many people, especially students.
- God warns against laziness because it is a refusal to exercise our God-given worth.
- Unemployment is crippling because it is an inability to exercise our worth.
- There is a battle to find meaning and God's perspective in the work we're involved with.

Campfire

Discuss together what the mountains mean and the ones that are particularly hard for you to climb. Can you describe the part your A-levels will play in any future plans you have? Or are they just a step in getting you to university?

Getting to university opens doors. It also requires work. A major challenge for today's A-level students is the increased range in the number of distractions brought by the techno interruptions – e.g. mobiles, online games, Facebook etc. The list is becoming increasingly long and varied.

What are the two biggest distractions you're prone to that prevent work being done and how can you combat them?

1. _____

2. _____

Work is a blessing

Adam's work was in the form of ruling and subduing. This command for Adam to work was given before humanity was corrupted by sin and is given as part of a blessing. Through working hard we are to gain satisfaction from work in the same way that God does. One of the effects of the fall was that work brought with it drudgery. However, it is still God's desire that work will bring us satisfaction.

Tent

Reflect on a time when you have worked really hard at a job or a task that you completed and that brought satisfaction to you. Maybe a DIY project, making an outfit, building a camp, completing coursework, learning to drive, caring for an animal, a sporting event you trained for…

Write in the box why it was satisfying:

Wisdom Box

Work is Spiritual

For the Christian all work is spiritual. A common misunderstanding and unhelpful perspective is that there is a division between those who work for the Church or Christian organisations – which is deemed spiritual work – and others whose work is seen as secular.

As we have seen we are all called to a work place and that work should have its place in everyone's life. It is our attitude to work that determines whether it is spiritual and brings glory to God. It could be paid work, voluntary work or homework!

> *'Whatever you do, work at it with all your heart, as working for the Lord, not for men.'*

> (Colossians 3:23 NIV)

Rope

Discuss ways in which you can honour God in the following places of work: a construction site, child care at home, a police station, a shop, the lecture hall, the stock market.

Excellence – giving our best

God is a worker par excellence; in offering our whole lives and work as worship to Him we are to follow His example in giving of our best. Excellence in the world is based on competition, which can be healthy but which also often leads to envy, greed, malice and even crime. It is based purely on comparative performance. There is a subtle difference between biblical and worldly excellence. The writer Mark Greene defines biblical excellence as this:

> *'Biblical success is not running faster than anyone else. It's running the best time you can - with God's help'*

What does it look like for you to give your best?

God loves and rewards excellence. Excellence opens doors. Remember Joseph! Now read the parable of the talents.

Lakes

Read Mathew 25:14-30

God wants us to use the gifts He's placed in us to develop our potential and to work in such a way that we are conscious and open to His involvement. Each of us is unique for a reason. The gifts you have are precious to God. They require nurturing, hard work and patience in order to develop them so that you might fulfil God's plans and purposes for your life.

Compass

- What are your talents?
- What steps should you take to develop them over the next 5 years?
- What will they look like when you are 30?

What is God saying to you?

Wisdom Box

Prayer

Father God, you are the most creative, compassionate, organised and hard working being there is! We thank you for choosing to partner with us. Help us to steward the gifts you've given well so that we might honour you with excellence. Amen.

Landscape: Friendships

BUILDING AUTHENTIC COMMUNITY

On starting university it's important to make friends. This chapter explores what it is to be a friend to people and to receive their friendship back, and it also highlights some of the difficulties and barriers we have in developing deep and meaningful friendships.

On arriving at university Mike recalls being in a poor mental state:

> 'The first day as I settled into halls my new neighbour knocked on the door with his dad in tow and said, "Hello my name is James. I'm next door." I replied, "That's nice" and shut the door. I wasn't happy. By the night of the Fresher's ball I was physically sick and sat staring at the ceiling alone. I quickly earned the nickname 'The Hermit' after getting up early and exercising then closing my door at nights.
>
> This behaviour began to have a bizarre effect though. I think by the grace of God (and the fact that I do enjoy the banter and fun company brings) those around me became intrigued by my behaviour and wanted to know more about me. As time went on individuals would come round, running with me in the early morning or dropping by for an evening chat. By the final week of the first term my room was being used for film nights. As I sat there surrounded by a bunch of sweaty students munching their way through take-out pizza I recall being altogether more satisfied with life…'

The deepest human need is to know and be known.

The connected life

Friendships are of utmost importance to God. Every page of Scripture describes some sort of relationship. Cultivating right relationships is God's number one priority and He desires that our lives should be connected with Him and other people.

We are made in the image of a communal God (Father, Son and Holy Spirit), a God who has experienced the very best of a loving, self-giving relationship and wants this to be our experience too. Being made in His image means that we have a longing for community and inclusion; we're meant to have mates, it's the way we're designed. Ask people what they value most about their friends and they'll probably say something along the lines of 'They are always there for me.'

Tent

Think about the people you consider to be your friends and write their friendship characteristics in the box below:

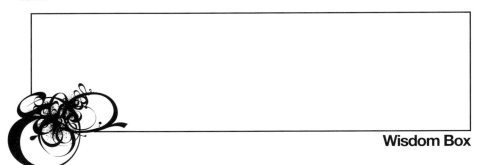

Wisdom Box

Friendship at University

Our culture has a loneliness epidemic but this is opposite to how God created us to be. Loneliness is one of the biggest-felt needs at university and many people miss out on the friendships and community they are made for. We want to explore what it takes to build the bridges of lasting friendship and open ourselves up to the possibility that during our journey through studentscape we can and will make friends for life.

Campfire

When in your life have you experienced loneliness? How did you respond?

Travelling companion

Ruth is going to help teach us about friendship. Her story is of God working out His purposes through a young woman who starts life as an outsider but chooses to honour her relationship to God and her mother-in-law. Her name in Hebrew actually means 'friendship' and she displays qualities of faithfulness, kindness and respect. It is a story of friendships forged under difficult circumstances.

Lakes

Read Ruth 1

Naomi is a godly Israelite woman and a widow. Life has been difficult and she plans to return alone to her people. However Ruth, a Moabite (a people at odds with Israelites), is determined to serve Naomi. Verses 16-17 suggest Ruth had a deep commitment and friendship with Naomi and she declares her loyalty and shares her expectations. Perhaps Ruth senses the spirit of God in this journey. In doing this Ruth is walking towards danger and a land full of potential enemies. Her loyalty is the mark of true friendship.

Campfire

Loyalty is hard to come by today, whether it is to a job, football team, church or marriage partner. The living out of commitments is what makes loyalty possible.

Discuss what it means to be loyal and committed to someone. Share some examples from your own life or people you know.

Mountains

'Though friendship is not quick to burn, it is explosive stuff'

(May Sarton)

Expectations, disappointments, conflict

Humans are complex beings, each of us with a unique background composed of millions of experiences. When we meet new people we make thousands of subconscious judgements and a few conscious ones in the first five minutes as part of our social interaction. A short meeting means you have already formed an impression and conclusions about the person, which are far beyond what you have discussed.

We create many expectations that have never been agreed or discussed and as friendships develop conflict almost certainly arises. Many friendships fail because expectations have never been communicated and disappointment or conflict has never been dealt with. Getting through this is the key to deep friendships and ones that stand the test of time. If we sweep issues under the carpet we will trip over them at a later date.

Take some time to write down some words that build friendship and some words that destroy friendship.

Build friendship...

Destroy friendship...

Wisdom Box

19

Streams

The Enemy's strategy is to destroy relationships. Conflicts can arise from Enemy strategy and attack friendships using control, jealousy, the holding of grudges, mistrust and gossip. Other destructive forces in us such as past hurt or rejection, difficulty in talking about deeper issues, fears, and character and personality traits can also damage true friendships.

Take a moment to prayerfully consider if you have or are prone to having any of the traits that destroy friendship. Circle them and pray about them, asking for God's help to change.

control	jealousy	holding of grudges
mistrust	gossip	past hurt/ rejection
character and personality traits	talking about deep secrets	fears

Rope

Can you think of a friend who is currently taking up too much of your headspace with negative thoughts? Are there role plays running through your mind in which you say exactly what you want to them, letting them know how wrong they are?

Fortunately there is some wisdom and a way out. The Bible is clear about what you need to do – Matthew 18:15 is the method. This will take courage and it will involve a risk. Go in humility and gentleness and speak privately to them and explain what it is they've done to hurt you or where you disagree. Be ready to listen to their side of the story as getting the wrong end of the stick is a common human trait!

Ruth demonstrated that being faithful in relationships is hard and it demands courage. This is true, even and especially in the church, where there is often pressure to be 'nice' and settling for pseudo-relationships. What does this mean? Well, it's not rocking the boat; it's sweeping 'stuff' under the carpet and faking it. In short, it's settling for mediocrity and a 'polite' smile. To break into authentic friendships we need gutsy honesty, humility and boldness. We need to confront hypocrisy in others and ourselves in a godly way to pave the way for real and healthy relationships.

Speaking the truth is tough. John Ortberg notes:

> *'There is a very important theological distinction between being a prophet and being a jerk. What burns deeply in the heart of a true prophet is not just anger but love.'*

True friendship is formed in fires. It is not a feeling. Too many people are fair weather friends. Loyalty is a commitment to be there for someone even when the going gets tough. It's where our friends can see the compassion of Jesus and where our love for people is not conditional.

Campfire

Discuss how you can be loyal to a friend even when they mess up because of values and behaviour that you don't agree with.

Lakes
Read Ruth Chapter 2

Ruth rocks up in Bethlehem with Naomi. She takes to the fields, wanting to serve her mother-in-law. However, there is no telling what may happen. Ruth's personal safety is precarious. The word has spread around the community that she is loyal. In verse 11 Boaz affirms her love and kindness.

Sometimes the journey can be hard going and a long slog. Our fellow travellers can be down and those around can be tired, especially at the end of the first term at university. In hard times acts of kindness like those Ruth shows to Naomi in verse 18 move relationships and community onto a new level. They become something that God can use to draw people to himself.

Friendships in community

The impact of godly relationships can affect a whole community. The opportunities for your relationships to impact the student world are huge. By visiting www.fusion.uk.com you can find out how you can start or be part of such a community.

Fusion Cells exist to be communities where our relationship with God and one another go deeper. They immerse themselves in the heart of the culture and follow Christ's example. Around Jesus, community broke out and He was labelled 'a friend of sinners'. God isn't exclusive in His friendships and neither should we be. He is always extending the hand of friendship.

Tent

Friendship is something we give yet we can only receive it when it is given to us. If we try and force friendship we end up manipulating people. Don't demand friendship - just be a friend.

Friendship is a gift that you can give away. Spend some time thinking about how you make your friendship available to others now and during your time at university. What aspects of friendship do you need to work on?

What is God saying to you?

Wisdom Box

Prayer
Lord Jesus, thank you for your friendship to us. Help us to create the kind of friendships that glorify you and to extend our friendship to others, especially those who don't know you. Amen.

Landscape: Lifestyle Pressures

The prevailing current of modern day student culture is a strong one and if you enter the water naively, you're likely to get swept away. There are many pressures on our lifestyle and expectations in student culture that conflict with who we are and how God desires us to live.

Words like 'now', 'I' and 'choice' reflect life at the start of the 21st century. 'Now' suggests the immediacy with which we would like service, food, career advancement and status. Technological advancement and media have fed a 'you can have it all today' mentality.

'I' could also be 'me' or 'my' and the individual approach to life, rights and fulfilment is breeding a very selfish society. 'Choice' is the big playground out there and choices are being made with very few limits and boundaries. Consequence is a distant after-thought with pleasure and convenience top priorities.

Life in the fast lane

'Upon entering university students have complete autonomy in a hedonistic culture'

(Matt Stuart)

Autonomy is the ability to choose what you do. There is nothing right or wrong in autonomy; it's merely the freedom to exercise choice. Upon entering the studentscape years, especially if you're leaving home for the first time there are more choices to make and a huge amount of freedom in exercising them.

Tent

University is life in the fast lane: it goes quickly, it's exhilarating, it's fun, and it's potentially dangerous. It demands lots of fast reactions to the supermarket of choices. Write down below some of the opportunities and challenges that you are anticipating at university.

Wisdom Box

Travelling companion

We are going to learn this month with Peter and look at an account in his life that required tough choices and bold actions. Peter was a passionate follower of Christ and often did and said things without thinking. In this account God decides to take Peter aside and show him something that would mean making difficult choices and would lead to the gospel breaking out into every culture.

Lakes
Read Acts 10:1-21

Widening our worldview

Peter is under pressure to stay within the Jewish sub-culture and not live for God, with and among a people who don't share his values. God offends him by asking that he eat 'unclean' food. He soon realises that what applied to food applied to people and that he shouldn't call 'unclean' what God has called 'clean'.

Now consider your own worldview and culture. What are your values and why?

> *'A value is something that consciously or subconsciously motivates and influences our decision making or choices.'*

A way of recognising what you value is by looking at your life and seeing how much time you spend on certain activities, things and people. Our life gets organised around these things – they are the things we value. Focus on your spare time when you're not sleeping, studying. Write down your main values.

1. _____

Why? _____

2. _____

Why? _____

3. _____

Why? _____

Hopefully, your values reflect something of Christ's values and your identity is found in who you are becoming, not in what you do or have. By asking why you are examining your motives.

Mountains

Here's the crunch. Following Jesus is a choice! Over the first few weeks of university many people who have professed a faith during their childhood and teenage years will sadly get blown away and lost in the crowd, and they'll opt out!

This can be for a number of reasons, so we're going to take a look at preparation – choices that you can make before you go.

'Fail to prepare, prepare to fail'

(Abraham Lincoln)

How we use our freedom is related to how we see ourselves and where our identity lies. As a Christian you need to know how loved you are by God and how much God delights in you. You belong to Him and nothing can change that. You can't get unloved or earn a little more love.

Autonomy or freedom of choice is God's invention – He wants us to choose right choices because we value relationship with God and others, not because we have to. University, at times, may feel like an assault on your identity and be quite disorientating. You are going to need to decide how you will handle this new found freedom before it happens. You will have to live in the culture and embrace some new customs but also recognise the customs that conflict with God's values.

Campfire

Below are some pressure areas on your identity that you will face at university. Write down how you will deal with them.

To have sex

Drink too much

Waste time

Spend more money

Internet Porn

To stop attending church

'Dark and difficult times lie ahead. Soon we must all face the choice between what is right and what is easy'

(J K Rowling, Harry Potter and the Goblet of Fire)

24

Compass

It will be easier and more appropriate if you do this exercise with friends of the same gender. If you feel God pointing to something really specific let your mates know. If you are not comfortable speaking to your mates, then go and speak to your youth or church leader

.Identify two pressures you currently face on a weekly basis. It will help if you are specific:

For example: 'Drinking' is ok but a little vague. Try saying, 'My mates calling me boring or religious if I refuse to have more than two drinks etc and it causes me to fear being left without friends.'

Discuss this. Attempt to work out specific fears that could affect your decision making in the moment when out with friends. By being specific with your fears through talking and prayer you are starting the disarming process: try it now!

Pressure 1_____

Pressure 2_____

2.Try setting a target for your first term at university. It might seem a long way off but you may be able to start implementing some things now. For example, maybe to not drink for that term or to stay single for the first term. This is wise and potentially a really helpful starting block for healthy, respectful relationships at uni. Others will know your boundaries and come to respect you for them.

Be honest with yourself - this is tough! What are your weaknesses? We all respond in different ways to pressure, (which you will be experiencing at times as a fresher). You may seek affection in unhelpful ways, or be prone to one more drink.

Streams

Pray together now over the current pressures you face. Ask for God's help and that you will be fully prepared when you face those pressures at university.

Lakes

Read Acts 10:22-48

Discovering God's Heart

Peter is walking down a road of discovery here. He is realising that God's desire to reach a lost world is greater than our desire to stick with what or who we know. One of the greatest hindrances to mission in the universities today is that of Christians who spend most of their time in meetings with other Christians.

You can be different. Will you be open to hanging out in the culture with those who don't share your values but remain 100% committed to God? You might be there already. Either way, over the next few months be open to God equipping you to be someone who can make tough choices and readily share your faith.

Write down the names of three people in your weekly activities who you'd like to share your faith with before venturing off to university.

1. _____

2. _____

3. _____

Lakes

Read Acts 11:1-18

Running with others

In Acts 11 the early Church is still ignorant to Christ's call to the Gentiles and Peter is called to accoun for entering Cornelius's house. However, Peter's revelation and experience brings to them a fulle understanding of God's purposes.

Having other Christians around us is vital. It ensures we stay accountable, humble and should als challenge our developing theology and lifestyle. Just look: nearly the whole of the early church had wrong! One guy gets his worldview challenged by God and the course of history is changed!

As hard as some people try, you can't be friends with everyone all the time. We need to prioritise. Jesu priority whilst here on earth was the twelve disciples. Of those twelve three were especially close with hir – Peter, James and John. John was his best mate (see John 13:23 – imagine that!).

Campfire

Having a few mates who are passionate about following Jesus is crucial if you are going to be sustained stay sharp and develop into the man or woman of God you've been called to be! You will need friends wh will be there for you as you run your race through uni & beyond!

Who are you prioritising time with now?

Think about how you will find someone who will be able to play that role when you are at uni.

These important relationships rarely just happen. They need to be cultivated. A way of widening the ne is to get along to a church. Do some homework before you go, take at look at the Fusion website www fusion.uk.com for churches and student cell groups in your university city.

What is God saying to you?

Wisdom Box

Prayer

Lord God, when I feel the squeeze of society please grant me the courage to stand firm so you might us it to mould me for your purposes. Amen.

Landscape: Spiritual Growth

WHO AM I BECOMING?

University years can be an opportunity for rapid spiritual growth. Cruise control is not an option and reverse doesn't work: we want to help you find top gear.

The Eagle

Once a farmer found an abandoned eagle's nest. In it was an egg that was still warm. He took the egg back to his farm and laid it in the nest of one of his hens. The egg hatched and the baby eagle grew up along with the other chickens. It pecked about the farmyard, scrabbling for grain. It spent its life within the yard and rarely looked up. One day, when it was very old, it lifted up its head and saw above it a wonderful sight – an eagle soaring high above in the sky. Looking at it, the old creature sighed and said to itself, 'If only I'd been born an eagle…'

Spiritual growth is a bit like this; if we are to soar we need to spend time looking up. However, measuring our spiritual growth by the number of 'quiet times' and 'disciplines' we undertake is too simplistic and essentially unhelpful. If we want to grow closer to God our motives need to dictate our methods. When we get down on our knees it isn't just our words God hears but He sees what is going on in our hearts. It is growing our relationship with God that we are going to focus on.

Spiritual fitness

I've been challenged to look at the condition of my life compared to the life I want to lead. I've realised that although my life oozes with the grace of God it is, in many areas, impoverished and lacking. As we explore spiritual growth we are not looking to get all the answers or even understand what the destination should look like. However, we will discover a few keys that will help us get the most out of the journey and have confidence in the next step.

'Spend your time and energy in training yourself for spiritual fitness'

(1 Timothy 4:7)

27

Mountains

We need to be spiritually fit if we are going to climb over the mountains that prevent us from growing spiritually. These mountains are the things that block or hinder your growth in God. Can you identify three mountains in your life that you feel hinder your spiritual growth?

1. _____

_____

2. _____

_____

3. _____

_____

Tent

Let's pause for a moment to consider our spiritual fitness. How fit do we think we are? Are we exercising our muscles with a few spiritual disciplines or piling on the pounds through gorging on a diet of TV soaps, reality TV and media gossip. Do we feel guilty or hypocritical about our lives?

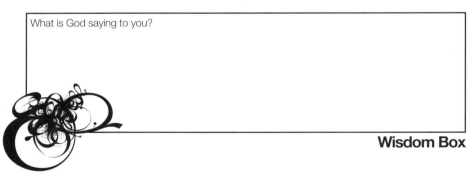

What is God saying to you?

Wisdom Box

God loves us and doesn't condemn us. He urges us to fill our lives with things that will cause us to spiritually soar with the eagles rather than just be satisfied with chicken feed!

Travelling Companion

Our travelling companion this month was familiar with difficult terrain and, as a 17 year old, was learning a lot about spiritual growth. Timothy is his name and he is best known and described through the letters of Paul. Paul's letters to him are packed with pearls of wisdom to encourage and develop Timothy in his growth into Christ-likeness.

Lakes

Read 1 Timothy 1:18 – 2:6

It is clear Timothy has some battles on his hands. When battles are fought well they are often times of considerable spiritual growth. For battles to be fought well there need to be some basic things in place. Paul mentions confidence, faith in Christ and a clear conscience as being foundational.

As you prepare for studentscape ask what do these three things mean for you.

1. Confidence   _____

2. Faith in Christ   _____

3. A clear conscience _____

First of all pray

Prayer is the doorway to relationship with God. It is our prayer 'lives' rather than our prayer 'times' that matter. Often prayer 'times' are used as an unhelpful barometer with regards to how we're going with God. Prayer is ultimately something that a Christian will be engaged in because talking with God is important if you want to walk into all He has for you.

However, many Christians just aren't really sure they're 'getting through' or doing it right when it comes to praying.

> *'And pray in the Spirit on all occasions with all kinds of prayers and requests'*

(Ephesians 6:18 NIV)

Prayer – permanently online

This varied prayer is our spiritual oxygen for each day. It keeps us in tune with the Spirit. I'm talking about a continuous connection with our Father in Heaven so heart cries, emotions, jokes and banter can be uploaded and downloaded at anytime. This free and unrestricted access to the throne room of God serves to tenderise our heart and keep us responsive to the activity of heaven on earth through the Holy Spirit. The majority of prayer is not so much a discipline as a way of life.

However, there are helpful exercises that can help develop prayer as a way of life and serve to enhance our times of solitude and silence. We must keep asking with the disciples 'Lord, teach us to pray.' Focused time given to intercession for friends and situations may demand us to stop what we are doing in order to align our body, mind and being to specific prayer. Keeping a prayer diary or journal not only helps us to pray but provides markers for answers to prayer that will build faith and keep us praying.

Campfire

How do you feel about your prayer life right now? Write down three words that describe it.

1. _____

2. _____

3. _____

Discuss the following together

- Do you find it easy being alone and still with God?
- Do you pray alone much, if at all?
- Where do find yourself speaking with God on a regular basis? In your bedroom, walking around town, out in the countryside, in a cell group?

Lakes

Read 1 Timothy 3:1-13

Write down in the box below all the positive values from these verses that demonstrate spiritual growth.

Wisdom Box

Campfire

Spiritual growth that results in us being able to take on responsibility in God's church clearly doesn't happen overnight. Ability and character need to be tested time and time again (see verse 10).

Can you identify a recent event in your life where your character has been tested? How did you fare?

_____

_____

_____

The good news is that we can't fail these tests in God as He is committed to forming and shaping us into His image. We can retake the test as many times as we need to. The danger is that we don't recognise when a life event is something that God wants to use to hone us and instead, we end up resisting the internal change.

Rope

Look at the box again and write down three areas of growth that you need to work on and how that growth could take place. For example, if you are greedy for money then find ways of giving it away and developing generosity.

1. _____

How? _____

2. _____

How? _____

3. _____

How? _____

Lakes

Read 2 Timothy 1:5-8 and 2:1-7

Fan into flames

There is good news for our spiritual growth. Not only has God given you a spiritual gift, He has also imparted to you power, love and self discipline in order that you have the inner strength and desire to grow.

Tent

Read over this passage from 2 Timothy 1 again and spend some time listening to God. In order to grow effectively in God we need to learn to be still with God and become more spiritually self-aware.

What spiritual gifts has He given you and how might you use them at university?

_____

_____

_____

Soldiers, athletes and farmers

Paul now packs in a load of metaphors for Timothy to think about and gain understanding from God. Write down one aspect from each metaphor that you can apply to your spiritual growth.

Soldier_____

Athlete_____

Farmer_____

Compass

'I have fought the good fight, I have finished the race, and I have remained faithful.'

(2 Timothy 4 7 NLT)

Paul's final remarks to Timothy include the above boast. He is facing the final straight of his life and he is awaiting his prize. It is important for Timothy to hear this from an old man who has no regrets for living his life wholeheartedly for God. Like Timothy we can look to the future with confidence and give ourselves fully to God's agenda, and know that every bit of spiritual growth brings us closer to the prize!

What is God saying to you?

Wisdom Box

Prayer

Father God I commit myself to growing more like your Son. Help me to be spiritually fit in order that I can maximise my spiritual growth. Teach me what it means to stay submitted to Christ in every area of life and to keep my eyes on the prize. Amen.

Landscape: Hard times

THE FIRES OF LIFE

ry few students go through university without encountering hard times. Hard times are part of life on rth and understanding how God is with us and for us during those times will help us stay close to God d walk through them.

ictory anyone?

Christians we may hear phrases like 'living the victorious Christian life' but often our life seems very removed from that victorious reality. It is sometimes difficult to find the balance between expecting d's power and victory to intervene into our situations, and also in being people who are real about our uggles, disappointments and hard times.

'Life is hard, but God is with us and heaven is real'

(Billy Graham)

s impossible to measure God's victory in our lives through our health, material wealth and status. God arches much deeper within and looks much further ahead to a new day. In the meantime we are stuck owing that Jesus has won the victory for us and our full inheritance awaits us.

this chapter we want to try and make a bit more sense of what it means to respond to a good God in e face of hard, tragic or even evil times.

ent

at has been the hardest time of your life so far?

_____

_____

_____

y was this time so hard?

_____

_____

We don't need to go looking for hard times. If we are alive we will face them. The world is not as it shou or shall be. In the meantime God calls us to live in this tension and whilst the Bible doesn't promise remove us from hard times, God promises to be with us in hard times. We are to pin our hopes on a ne day – Heaven.

Travelling Companion

We are taking an event from the life of Hannah to discover more about what it means to live and respor to God when life doesn't work out the way we want. Hannah had the stigma of being barren in a cultu where to have no children was a source of disgrace. She's honest with God and through bitter tears sh chooses to honour God and follow through with more hard choices.

Lakes

Read 1 Samuel 1

Peninnah is quick to provoke and irritate Hannah. It stems from jealousy because Hannah is Elkanah's fir love. Her words are aimed to oppress and hurt Hannah.

Is there someone in your past or present that has taunted you, bullied you or generally made your li miserable? What has been your response? Look at the word boxes below. Circle three words per box.

Internally, what goes on?

Hurt	Anger	Cry out to God
Fear	Role plays	Self pity
Anxiety	Revenge	Self hate

Externally, how do you respond?

Gossip	Talk it through	Withdrawal
Lobbying	Tell others	Rage outbursts
Fight them	Avoidance	Challenge them

Campfire

Take some time to share your experiences.

'Life's not fair'

It is clear that life isn't fair. There isn't the justice there should be in the world – we only have to watch fi minutes of the news to remember that life on this planet is full of heartache.

Deep down do you expect life to be fair to you, or do you accept that life isn't fair?

Hannah's response

Hannah reached a place where her life had become unbearable. She'd long since reached her end wi regards to her situation. She was letting it all hang out before God… see 1 Samuel 1:10.

Have you ever cried bitterly to God? If so, what was it over?

ent

your hard times how do you know God still cares? How do you respond to him?

ke some time to listen to what God thinks and feels about some of the tough times in your life.

tice how Hannah is encouraged by Eli and how her husband Elkanah walks the journey with her.

hat part do others play in your life struggles?

_____

_____

you ask for help? If not, why?

_____

_____

he Two Wolves

Native American grandfather was talking to his grandson about how he felt. He said, 'I feel as if I ve two wolves fighting in my heart. One wolf is the vengeful, angry, violent one. The other wolf is the ing, compassionate one.' The grandson asked him, 'Which wolf will win the fight in your heart?' The andfather answered: 'The one I feed.'

r response in any given situation feeds who we are becoming.

t's be clear, the hard times in our lives are not instigated by God as a way of punishing us into line. wever, depending on how we choose to respond to the very things that have hurt us and caused us in means they can become the fire of God. God in His infinite wisdom, creativity and love for us can use m to reveal some of the deep truths of God to us, about where our identity really lies and where our e home really is.

Rope

eeing beyond the pain

aven is our home and part of our gaze needs to be fixed there. Many people believe in heaven but it es revelation to take this belief and make it a living hope.

> 'If you read history you will find that the Christians who did most for the present
> world were precisely those who thought most of the next. It is since Christians
> have largely ceased to think of the other world that they have become so
> ineffective in this.'

(C.S. Lewis)

s the assurance of Heaven that means Christians can respond differently to hard times. However, this elation of Heaven needs to be sought and the Bible is clear that we are to 'Set our sights on Heaven d let Heaven fill our thoughts' (Colossians 3:1-2).

Below are four barriers to heavenly thinking:

MATERIALISM – you like your stuff too much: gadgets, car, computer, clothes. Buying things bring comfort, rather than thinking about the God of all comfort and our future comfort in heaven.

PRIDE – you live for yourself, your success and fame. You work to create your reward here on earth. Yc live independently from God and see no need for Heaven as you are creating your own heaven here c earth without God's help.

FEAR – this can be any fear that limits and restricts, especially fear of death. Fears might reveal some co beliefs that deep down we don't believe Heaven is real or that God loves us. Lies are closely connecte with fears.

SATISFIED NOW – you prefer the foretaste of Heaven available here on earth and never think abo reward, judgement, Heaven, Hell or life after death.

Campfire

Spend some time talking about how you view Heaven and share if this hope of Heaven has ever helpe you through hard times.

We all have barriers to heavenly thinking. Look at the four barriers above and see if any stand out. Wri down in the box below what God is saying to you.

What is God saying to you?

Wisdom Box

Abandoned Prayer

Hannah is bitter but there is no mention of her sinning. Instead she makes a vow to God. A vow is prayer of binding agreement with God. It abandons future events and choices to God. Hannah can do th because deep down she believes in the goodness of God.

Hannah could have done any number of things but she trusts and is patient. She's rewarded with a sc who becomes a nation's spiritual leader during a time of need. Hannah knew that Heaven was real ar this enabled her to fulfil her vow by giving Samuel away for God's glory.

Write down what you envisage being hard at university

s you consider those future events and circumstances, what decisions can you make now for how you ill respond to them?

or example – I will draw on friendships and let others in or I will choose to abandon myself to God, trusting at He will hold me.

_____

_____

_____

ter Hannah had done business with God she trusted that He'd heard her abandoned prayer. Hannah uld have done any number of things but she is no longer sad (she trusts God and cheers up), she eats sign of her anxiety giving way to peace and hunger) and she sleeps with her husband (she plays her art).

Streams

alking about hard times and heaven provokes all kinds of reactions and emotions in us. Spend some time aying with one another and listening to God. Use the prayer below if helpful.

What is God saying to you?

Wisdom Box

Prayer

esus, thank you for my life. I want to live for you and respond to you whatever comes my way. Help me to ee my life from your perspective, and please help Heaven to become more of a reality in my mind and life. trengthen me for life's tough times and sustain me with your presence when they come along. Amen.

Landscape: Holistic Lifestyle

LIFE RHYTHMS

Each new life stage demands new life rhythms. University presents a fantastic opportunity for great understanding about how you are wired and how you can get the most out of the marathon of life. The guy who started the running boom in America during the 1970's, Bill Rodgers, gives an elite perspective to approaching a marathon:

'Racing is all about rationing your resources'

This sounds simple, like common sense really! Sadly, many people live in ongoing struggle, trying to get on top of the things that make up their life. Christians are not exempt from this and are, arguably, more prone to projecting an outer togetherness while harbouring inner turmoil. To run the race that is marked out for us our lives need to be sustainable. By putting some good rhythms and practices into our lives now the risk of burn out, breakdown or backsliding are kept a long way off.

Can you think of a time in your life where you were constantly rushing or felt out of control? What were the pressures you faced?

Mountains

Just living in this world adversely affects our spiritual sharpness. Circle three things that affect you when you feel under pressure.

Always late	Forget things	Sleep struggles	Miss opportunities
Don't listen	Eat standing up	Speak fast	Lose things
Quiet time cut	Road rage	Irritable	Preoccupied

To pick up on Bill Rodgers' point, in order to run the race effectively we need to know what resources we can have and how to use them. Everyone is different and has a different capacity for output. Our capacity can change with a different life stage or experience. It is likely that whilst at university you'll be stretched to new limits and be around people of different capacity and competence. It is worth noting at this point that comparing ourselves with others invariably leads to problems.

Travelling Companion

Daniel is a new student and away from home for the first time and he is going to help us learn more about a holistic lifestyle. The choices Daniel makes as a young man are foundational for the great old man that faces the lions. Daniel is a fantastic example of someone who takes life rhythms seriously. He shows us how to live for God in a very hostile land and when to challenge the cultural values of his adopted nation.

Lakes

Read Daniel Chapter 1

Campfire

Write down five words that describe Daniel

1. _____

2. _____

3. _____

4. _____

5. _____

Daniel belongs to an elite group. In this way there are some similarities to modern day students studying in Britain. He is a young intellectual with potential to influence the influencers (the King). Similarly, the Christian students of today are in a great position to become or influence the CEOs of tomorrow.

Daniel possesses social skills and leadership potential. University is a great place to serve a foundational apprenticeship in Christ. It is a place to be sharpened by a diverse range of mentors and a place to gain valuable leadership skills and life experience.

Tent

Verse 5 notes that the young men served a three year training period before the 'crème de la crème' were selected for service in the royal courts.

Have you considered your three years at university as your potential spiritual training ground? Ask God about some of the things He wants you to learn.

What is God saying to you?

Wisdom Box

Exercising restraint

As a prisoner in a pagan land Daniel is offered food from the finest kitchen. This is a privilege he 'can refuse'. However, Daniel decides to have a restricted diet and exercise the discipline of abstinence. Why? Because eating unclean food would be to go against the Jewish Torah, which was God's law.

There will be times where we're suddenly faced with a moral dilemma. Those are the times when our true values and beliefs are revealed. For Daniel, it wasn't a decision to be made because he had already made it! He'd already sorted his priorities. Having order on the inside helps us make good choices and it can also prevent us from making wrong ones.

Campfire

Have you ever been faced with a moral dilemma?

If so, what happened?

_____

_____

What did you learn from that experience?

_____

_____

Rope

Capturing my time

Only some of the choices we make are moral ones i.e. good or bad. Often our choice for what to do with our time will be a choice between the good and the great offers. As a student you will enter a period of life where you will be inundated with offers. Next are three things to consider before we evaluate how your time is spent.

1.PRIORITISING

What are your priorities in life? When you look back over the last month are those priorities reflected? It is good practice to sit down once a year and set out your goals for the coming year. What do you want to achieve? What do you want to change? Encourage a friend to do the same and every three to four months take some time out to re-evaluate.

'Work first, play second'

This is a good and healthy principal to instil. It will improve the quality of both work and play and it means what needs to get done, gets done. The following diagram can help you in this.

IMPORTANT BUT NOT URGENT = PLAN	URGENT AND IMPORTANT = DO
NEITHER URGENT OR IMPORTANT = FILE	URGENT BUT NOT IMPORTANT = DELEGATE

(vertical axis: Important)
(horizontal axis: Urgent)

2.RESTING

Whenever possible use God's template of 'six on one off'. If this isn't possible then take two off the next week. Some wise words of warning:

'Every rest day skipped is a future sick day stored'

How do you spend your 'down' time?

_____

_____

By engaging with God and our surroundings during our down time we'll find we're being better nourished in the long term. More often than not try an alternative to turning the television on. You may be surprised to find how this is often more refreshing. During our resting hours we're still spiritually and emotionally receptive. Try substituting another programme for a game of chess, a walk somewhere peaceful or a board game with friends.

3.PLANNING TIME AHEAD

(You'll need to buy a diary). Diaries are fantastic tools if used wisely. We should never become enslaved t one but rather use it as an aid.

Current Evaluation

The pizza below is cut into eight slices. Each slice represents a part of your life. Shade in each slice with colouring pen up to the amount of time that that area currently has in your life.

The idea is not to fill every slice to the brim but for there to be a healthy balance across the different area You can then evaluate where your time is going and if you need to cut back on some activities and giv more attention to others.

Campfire

Having filled in the pizza spend a few minutes discussing why yours is filled in the way it is. Has anythin surprised you?

Write down below three areas that need some adjustment and what you intend to do.

1. _____

Action_____

2. _____

Action_____

3. _____

Action_____

Tent

Have you ever considered fasting? Daniel went on a partial fast of vegetables and water and it kept him spiritually sharp and in tune with God. Jesus said 'When you fast...' (Matthew 6:16 NIV) There is an expectation that as His followers we will fast.

Fasting isn't easy but it is designed to bring God's strength out of our weakness. It can bring us closer to God. Why not give it a go and miss a meal or two and spend the time worshipping, praying and listening to God instead.

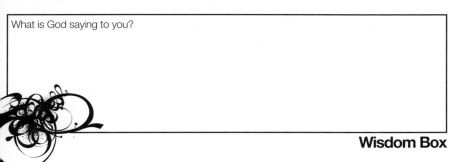

What is God saying to you?

Wisdom Box

Prayer

Lord God, help me find the right rhythm for my life so that I can be a blessing to you and to others. Help me make the right small choices everyday so that my lifestyle is sustainable and I can keep running fast for you. Amen.

Landscape: Stress

We've all been there with that feeling – the knot in your stomach is rising up into your throat, your palms are sweaty and your lips are dry. You want to go to the toilet; 'Surely I only went five minutes ago… this can't be right!' You feel sick but time has run out. The laughing dies down and the school falls silent. The Deputy Head beckons you forward. Fumbling with your piece of paper you begin the long walk onto the stage towards the microphone…

A recent survey found that public speaking was the number one fear amongst British adults. Whether it's acute fear or mild embarrassment, there are times when outside influences produce a turbulent sea of reactions inside our bodies. University can be a time of great stress, but before we go any further we need this to be clear:

'Stress is not what happens to you but what happens in you.'

Travelling Companion

Our friend this month is Esther. Born a Jew in a foreign land, Esther is orphaned at an early age. Initially she is a seemingly passive character yet when her circumstances change dramatically she enters the spotlight and has to deal with a number of stressful situations.

Lakes

Read Esther 1 and 2

Mountains

Perhaps you're having problems meeting an impending coursework deadline or need to speak to a friend about something they've apparently said about you. Maybe there are some unspoken expectations your parents have of your A-level results. These are all real situations facing many school leavers.

One of the best methods for dealing with stressful situations is to start by talking about them. This means speaking honestly with trusted friends about the things that won't be going away this year. Let's start by identifying the stressors (things that induce stress) in our lives.

Campfire

Discuss in your group the three biggest challenges you've faced over the past six months and list them (most challenging first):

For example: Relationships – Time management – Making Decisions

Biggest challenges faced:

1. _____

2. _____

3. _____

Jot down what you feel you've learned from these experiences in the box below and what you could take from them into future situations:

Wisdom Box

Identify your biggest challenge over the next three months

_____

_____

Ever heard the phrase 'Time equals money'? Well, in business it invariably does! We live in a capitalist society where companies invest millions training staff to use their time more effectively so they can make more money! Handling stress is big business but if you can't handle the heat then it's out the kitchen door. To coin Alan Sugar's phrase, 'You're fired!'

Now, the other thing society sells us is the goal of independence. The media portrays independence as a sign of maturity. The message is clear: make it on your own. Work hard, build your empire and then you'll have made it… It's every man/woman for themselves!

Lakes

Read Esther 3 and 4

The Bible is clear that life is a team game. Each of us has a unique contribution to bring and while there are star players like Esther, we all have a vital role to play.

In these chapters Esther's situation isn't looking so rosy; she's stuck with an egotistical maniac for a husband who has an aptitude for making rash decisions. He's appointed a second in command who is evil and hell bent on massacring her people. This is all because Esther's nearest relative has stood up to him…but now he's got hours to live and the hopes of a nation rest on Esther's shoulders. On hearing this Esther 'was deeply distressed' (Esther 4:4 NLT)

Esther is soon faced with a series of choices if she is to save her people.

Tent

When we're tired and stressed our defences are at their weakest. It's often at this point when we do things that either hurt others or ourselves. Look at the word box below and circle three words you can identify with.

Snap	Passive	Irritable	Selfish
Negative	Tearful	Frustrated	Muddled
Forget	Lustful	Anxious	Compare

As these things occur what steps can you take to keep yourself from doing something you may later regret? How do our life rhythms play a part?

_____

_____

_____

_____

Lakes

Read Esther 5 and 6

Let's look at how Esther handles the situation:

Esther is proactive.

She takes a risk by entering the King's presence unannounced – the King could execute her for such a stunt (Esther 5:1-2). The key is that Esther did something! Procrastination in this situation would have been fatal! Procrastination can be debilitating and if left unchecked it threatens our destiny. We can procrastinate for reasons such as fear of failure, fear of what others might say, or laziness.

Tent

Do you find yourself procrastinating? Are you often 'doing' but then unsure of what it is you've actually got done? Do you ever get a vague nagging feeling as you have one more go on the PS3 or watch the next TV programme?

On the next page jot down things you find yourself doing when you ought to be working.

ist your own top three and add things from other people's experience.

_____

_____

_____

ther._____

Rope

uddy up with someone in the group and agree to be accountable about your number one way of rocrastinating. The aim is to nail it over the next few weeks. They say it takes six weeks to form a habit. y putting post-it notes in your work file or around your room. Challenge yourself. Do you really need to go nd make another cup of tea? Think! In six weeks you could have formed a new life skill that will release ur potential through university and beyond!

Esther understands the importance of correct timing.

ne pressure must be absolute as her nation's future is dependant on this meeting and yet Esther ostpones (Esther 5:4). The temptation to panic or rush must have been excruciating but Esther resisted nd put her faith and confidence in God.

nink of someone you know who exudes confidence. He or she seems to have the knack of saying the jht thing at the right time. What is it they do?

_____

_____

Esther trusts that God is involved.

od is looking to be involved when we trust Him – 'That night the king had trouble sleeping…' (Esther 6:1 LT). Mordecai and Esther find favour overnight in the king's eyes helping them to gain approval with their quest the next day.

Campfire

iscuss in your group how God has been faithful in a sticky situation.

Streams

/hile at times our walk can be lonely, God never designed us to take an individual journey. Make some ace and spend 10-15 minutes praying for each other. Consider your upcoming exams, balancing your orkload, unknown destinations in September and any specific requests your non-Christian mates may ave.

od doesn't promise us stress-free lives. Early Christians would have struggled to get life insurance – trips the amphitheatre tended to take place the wrong side of the barrier. Authentic Christian lives are lived ut in a messy and fallen world. This means there will be times when we'll run into the same problems just anyone else does. In the stresses of everyday life the key is to keep our focus on God and take time ut to refocus regularly. God promises that He will always be with us (Jeremiah 32:40) and will give us His eace (John 14:27).

Compass

Here are a couple of ideas for handling stress…

1. The two-minute stop

There are 1440 minutes in a day and you can't save any of them; you can only spend them more wisely. When you're next dashing around with a dozen things going on try an enforced stop of two minutes. Take 120 seconds just to stop, stay still, catch your breath and ask God for a fresh perspective.

2. The spiritual discipline of silence

Prayer is primarily about relationship. If we arrive at prayer time with a long list and one eye on the clock our prayer life will be in danger of becoming mechanical. Try sitting down for five minutes in a secret place. Start by stilling your mind and wait on God.

Revision time!

You've made it this far so now's good time to ask yourself why you're sitting these exams, what you are hoping to get out of doing them and how they will glorify God. Don't shrink back now – finish on strongly!

What is God saying to you?

Wisdom Box

Prayer

Lord God, may I find you to be the prince of peace when I am feeling anxious and help me to convey your peace to others when they are in distress. Amen.

Landscape: Self Discipline

SELF CONTROL AND SMALL CHOICES

With freedom comes responsibility. University is a time of great freedom and we want to explore some of the keys for making the most of this freedom, with the fun and fulfilment that it brings.

Discipline is a misunderstood word. For many young people it's a 'dirty' word conjuring up connotations of constraint and rules. Spiritual disciplines are potentially even more misunderstood. I used to see them as individualistic pursuits of holiness that were measured by time spent engaging in certain practices, often boring, lacking in fun and with a measure of guilt and condemnation thrown in.

Spiritual disciplines were supposed to equal a healthy spiritual life and that seemed to relegate the rest of life to being fun but not very spiritual. Those in the church didn't seem to be particularly benefiting from them and the popular culture ridiculed them. However, desperation and desire for something deeper caused me to reconsider some of my previous experience and I invite you to join me and revisit some ancient practices and dig again for spiritual treasure.

Tent

Consistent good choices can be found behind the lives of the most free-spirited, gregarious people and the overwhelming majority of people would agree that discipline is of value. Discipline is the small things we do when we're not feeling inspired. It is the making of good choices in view of what we know is right and is at times contrary to our feelings.

Think of someone you know who you would describe as a disciplined person. List three of their qualities or attributes below:

_____

_____

_____

How would score your own self-discipline out of 10? _____

Whatever you do...

If a Christian segregates their life into spiritual activities and non-spiritual activities it denies them the fullness of participation in the extravagant gift of life that God has given. To live means to bring glory to God through whatever activity we engage in (Colossians 3:17). Every activity has spiritual repercussions and is to be done for the glory of God. Therefore, spiritual disciplines can be seen as any life discipline we partake in that magnifies the life of Jesus in us. The whole of life is spiritual – a gift from God, who is Spirit – and has the capacity for every discipline we engage in to enhance our life and celebrate our relationship with God.

Travelling companion

The wise advice of Paul to the early Church and to Christians makes him a dependable travelling companion. Paul spent the first half of his life as a leading Pharisee and was used to living a strict lifestyle in accordance with the Jewish Torah (religious law). However, in an encounter with Christ on the road to Damascus, God opened his eyes to a new grace-filled life.

Lakes

Read 1 Corinthians 9:19-27

Willpower

It is so easy to let our emotions dictate our choices. When faced with a challenge it seems that most of us are predisposed to find the path of least resistance. The problem with this is that it is often through resistance and making choices that appear harder when we discover who we really are and what really matters in life.

Paul was someone who made decisions out of his will and not his emotions – he had willpower! He demonstrated the ability to choose right even when his feelings and emotions wanted something else.

Campfire

Discuss together two recent choices you have made, one that was based on willpower, the other that was based on feelings.

What were the consequences of those choices? How did they make you feel?

Free to respond

Discipline for the Christian is not about set structure or even a daily routine, but freedom, flexibility and obedience. However, part of our freedom means we work and live within certain parameters and boundaries. We are often tied up with our own agendas so discipline is there to remind us again of God's agenda. Disciplines that are woven into the fabric of daily living are our passage to freedom and fulfilment. The fruit of any Christ-centred discipline will be a greater responsiveness to the Holy Spirit.

> *'A disciplined person is someone who can do the right thing at the right time in the right way with the right spirit or motive'*

(J. Ortberg)

Mountains

God is primarily interested in our heart motive. It's our motive that will determine our attitude to different things in life and this will be evident in the way we go about our responsibilities and relationships. We could act like the real deal – doing the right things at the right time – but God looks at the heart.

Circle the things in each column you know are weaknesses in you.

Things we do	Time we spend	Ways we live	Motives we have
Work	Procrastination	Rushing	Fear of failure
Exercise	Getting side tracked	Not giving 100%	Sense of duty
Bible	Lying in bed	Begrudgingly	Pride
Diet	Other priorities	Selfishly	Want to be seen
Sleep	Forgetfulness	Overtired	Fear of people
Prayer	Television	Legalistically	Anxious

Campfire

Look at the word box above and talk about things from each of the columns that you have circled: things that could stop you from doing the right thing, at the right time, in the right way with the right motive.

Streams

Spend some time praying with friends into some of these areas and let God's grace and peace flood your life. There is help at hand from the Holy Spirit and others, and next we are going to look at a few grace gifts that help produce the right values and motives in us.

Rope

Giving, servanthood and abstinence are three areas of discipline that help form God's values in us and enable us to make good choices.

God is the most generous person I know. He gives eternal life, gives us His Son, and gives us the Holy Spirit. We are to reflect His character and nature and be generous too, not just in what we give, but the way in which we give. Therefore we should not be giving to be seen but instead we should give in faith, give cheerfully and give sacrificially.

The right heart motive behind the act of giving is what God is interested in. In Luke 21 the widow who gave just two coins of very small value was highly esteemed by Jesus for her sacrifice. We can't out give God with our money, our tithes or our offerings and in Malachi 3 God invites the people to test the Lord's generosity.

As we learn to give (especially when we are a student) it frees us from a love of material things and develops this value of generosity in us. Make a decision to give whilst being a student. Remember, if you can afford a beer, you can afford to give!

Servanthood is the way to knowing our identity in God; it is our passage to fulfilment and freedom. It cultivates sacrificial love in our heart and develops a Kingdom perspective. The discipline of service is a way to train ourselves away from pride, arrogance, envy, resentment or self pity. Jesus did not come to be served but to serve others (Matthew 20:28) and calls us all to follow in His footsteps to keep the service of others central to our lifestyle (Philippians 2:5-7).

Having the true heart of a servant means that any task or request asked of us at any time can be carried out with joy and fulfilment. As Henri Nouwen put it:

> *'Wherever we see real service we also see joy, because in the midst of service a divine presence becomes visible and a gift is offered.'*

We need to get a hold of the fact that God rewards the heart attitude.

> *'Work hard and cheerfully at whatever you do, as though working for the Lord rather than people. Remember the Lord will give you an inheritance as a reward, and the Master you are serving is Christ.'*

(Colossians 3:23-24)

To abstain for a time or season from parts of our life that have become familiar such as television, magazines, the gym, computers, alcohol, food or music allows us to gain a fresh focus on the priorities in our lives. It's not necessarily that these natural desires are bad; it is just an opportunity to curb excess indulgence and to free us from the smallest amount of addiction that may have crept in.

> *'By the carefully adapted arrangement of our circumstances and behaviour, the spiritual disciplines will bring these basic desires into their proper co-ordination and subordination within the economy of life in his Kingdom.'*

(Dallas Willard)

Campfire

Rate yourself on these specific areas. Give yourself a mark out of ten next to each one.

GIVING – Generosity vital   (Rating   /10)

SERVANTHOOD – On His Majesty's Secret Service   (Rating   /10)

ABSTINENCE – Ordering our priorities   (Rating   /10)

- How can you increase your rating in each area?
- What might these areas look like at your uni?

Keeping it simple

As a senior church leader Paul led a simple life. He earned his living as a tent maker. This was integral to his life work as it sustained him and undoubtedly gave him further opportunities to share the gospel.

Simplicity is not about stinginess and poverty but about true abundance. It is about opening time to create space and about everyday small choices. Ruth Valerio states,

> *'It's (partly) about our choices… what choices have we made that have led us to where we are… too often we're on the treadmill of life paying the consequences for choices we didn't even realise we had made.'*

Simple living within the kingdom of God is about being joyfully aware of what we do and why we do it – this means having a life objective.

If you are reading this then it is likely you are just discovering the contribution God created you to be for this world. Your whole working lives are ahead of you, which means you have around 1.8 billion more seconds to fill. Most of our small choices take less than a second to make but end up forming our character and our legacy.

Write down in three words or phrases how you would want your life to be remembered

1. _____

2. _____

3. _____

What is God saying to you?

Wisdom Box

Prayer

Father God, I thank you that you have a wonderful purpose for my life – that I should live for your glory. Help me to form habits and disciplines that mean I can make the right choices and be a blessing to you, others and myself. Amen.

Landscape: Celebration
THE ART OF PARTYING HARD

In John 10:10 Jesus promised us life to the full. His first miracle in Cana meant the party could continue. In following Christ at university we must learn how to celebrate who He is with our whole lives.

Celebration is a central part of a life lived to the full. We celebrate for a diverse number of reasons. Christmas, birthdays and anniversaries offer us the opportunity of sharing a special time together with those we love. These celebrations are landmarks in our lives. Often, they are the high points after a period of testing. Whether it's a sporting triumph, a company celebrating the completion of an arduous project or A-level students partying upon finishing their exams, celebration plays a vital role in our life rhythms.

Celebration brings about closure. It allows us to stop for a moment on a crest with our fellow travellers, glance back over the valley we've walked through before setting our sights on new ground. The 12-14 week space between school and uni is a unique time. Whether it's the big parties, a holiday abroad you've looked forward to or taking camping trips with mates, the opportunities for fun will be almost endless. But it's an important time too! The special occasions interspersed with down time allow our minds to relax freeing our emotions and creating a fresh outlook for the future.

Campfire

Can you remember a time of celebration that you particularly enjoyed?

What was it that made this event or time special to you?

Mountains

Hedonism

God is the creator of pleasure. It is His idea and God wants to be part of our wildest celebration. However, the devil is incapable of conjuring up pleasurable pursuits that celebrate who we are and instead twists healthy celebration into excesses that can damage others and us.

C.S. Lewis, in his fictional 'Screwtape Letters', has a senior demon giving advice to a nephew demon. Uncle Screwtape advises 'An ever-increasing craving for an ever-diminishing pleasure is the formula. Basically, hedonism will never satisfy.

Some students start nights out with the intention of having a good time. However, if there are no boundaries or reference points it can end up as self-absorbed hedonism. Boundaries are helpful as they help us to avoid overdoing it. Pursuing pleasure for its own sake is to miss the point of real celebration. God designed celebration in such a way that we'd be drawn closer to Him.

Campfire

What does hedonism look like in the people around you?

Can you identify what the roots to hedonism are?

Write in the box below any that are in you.

Wisdom Box

For some, parties can be intimidating. The danger here is that people are missing out due to shyness or because they feel they don't fit in. It is important to engage, even if it's not your natural tendency. By shunning the celebration process you are potentially missing out on being refuelled and rejoicing with those who rejoice.

Travelling Companion

This month we're camping with King David. He's recently been faced with challenges, a bit like yourselves. David has defeated the Jebusites to reclaim Jerusalem. Having been triumphant he decides to take the Ark of the Covenant back to his city. It is time to celebrate.

Lakes

Read 2 Samuel 6:1-11

Don't touch!

The celebrations turn ugly as the specific instructions on how to move the Ark of the Lord are ignored. A man dies because the respect for God is lost in the midst of the party. David spends the next three months seeking God on this. He is humbled and examines his motives with a fresh understanding of whom he's doing this for. As you look forward to your summer break what things can you put in place, or do, so that God starts as the central point to everything you engage in over the next few months.

1. _____

2. _____

3. _____

Lakes

Read 2 Samuel 6:12-22

David begins his celebrations with an awareness of God's greatness. He holds God in reverence. It is less about David and more about God. However, not everyone is in the mood for partying. David is not concerned about his image but Michal is filled with contempt and is more concerned with appearance than motives.

Tent

Whilst it is difficult to admit to identifying with Michal, sometimes we are not very good at rejoicing with those who rejoice. It is a form of envy that stops us sharing another person's joy. God wants to free us so we can look on other people with generosity.

Spend a few moments letting God search your heart and recall to mind any times where you have struggled to celebrate with others.

Rope

Help is at hand, below are three tools to help us celebrate God.

PARTY HARD - The Practice of Celebration

Celebration lifts us out of envy, comparison and bitterness and forms attitudes of thankfulness and gratitude in us. It causes us to wonder and dream again.

'You shall go out in joy, and be led forth in peace; the mountains and the hills will burst into song before you, and all the trees of the field will clap their hands.'

(Isaiah 55:12 NIV)

Out of the tithe that the Israelites offered once a year God gave these instructions for how a portion of it should be spent;

'When you arrive, you may use the money to buy any kind of food you want – cattle, sheep, goats, wine, or other alcoholic drink. Then feast there in the presence of the Lord your God and celebrate with your household'

(Deuteronomy 14:26 NLT)

Is this your image of God?

Campfire

Why not plan a celebration for all your friends at the end of exams. Discuss together how God's values can be central and how all your friends can feel part of the celebration.

JOY RIDING – The journey of following Jesus is to be filled with joy

'Joy is the serious business of heaven'

(C.S. Lewis)

We are heaven's representatives. If we don't rejoice today we never will. John Ortberg recommends having a 'Joy Mentor' for people who struggle to celebrate life, thus making sure they take time to hang around those people who make them feel good and are full of joy themselves.

To be full of joy is the inheritance of every follower of Christ; it is a journey to be taken with others.

'We want to work together with you so you will be full of joy as you stand firm in your faith.'

(2 Corinthians 1:24)

The result is:

'...even now you are happy with a glorious, inexpressible joy.'

(1 Peter 1:8)

Joy is the result of a life abandoned to loving and trusting God.

'We are invited to rejoice in every moment of life because every moment of life is a gift'

(J. Ortberg)

Write the name of your joy mentor here _____

Having a laugh

'Why not?! Jesus had a sense of humour – some of his parables are positively comical. There is even such a thing as 'holy laughter', a frequent phenomenon in various revival movements. Although I have not experienced holy laughter myself, I had observed it in others and its effects appear altogether beneficial. But whether God gives you this special grace or not, we can all experience wholesome laughter...'

'So poke fun at yourself. Enjoy wholesome jokes and clever puns. Relish good comedy. Learn to laugh; it is a discipline to be mastered. Let go of the everlasting burden of always needing to sound profound.'

(R.Foster)

Streams

Spend some time praying for each other to experience God's joy so that we can be bringers of joy to others.

A THANKFUL ATTITUDE – Holding onto the good

We will always be confronted with the bad, the negative, the cynical – it will always be there. This is not a denial of those things but rather an opportunity to be healed from them. A thankful attitude lifts us from self, whether it is from self-pity, selfishness, self-consciousness or self-sufficiency. The reason for our thankfulness is that God is good! Our thanks will increase as we focus on Him and the good things He has made and has for us to do. Paul exhorts us to 'Hold onto the good' (1 Thessalonians 5:21 NIV)

Thankfulness is a choice. You can't be thankful and miserable at the same time. The psalmist was always making the choice in all kinds of circumstances and declared, 'I will give thanks to the Lord!'

A note by the side of the bed can help remind us last thing at night and first thing in the day to be thankful to God. Make a list of what you are thankful for and weave the prayer of thanks into your working day so we can 'give thanks in all circumstances' (1 Thessalonians 5:18 NIV).

> *"To be grateful is to recognise the Love of God in everything He has given us – and He has given us everything. Every breath we draw is a gift of His love, every moment of existence is a grace, for it brings with it immense graces from Him. Gratitude therefore takes nothing for granted, is never unresponsive, is constantly awakening to new wonder and to praise of the goodness of God. For the grateful person knows that God is good, not by hearsay but by experience. And that is what makes all the difference."*

(T Merton)

To end this session write down as many things as you can in the box below that you are thankful for.

What is God saying to you?

Wisdom Box

Prayer

Incorporate some of the things in the box above in a prayer of thanks to God.

58

Landscape: Money, Money, Money

'Money, money, money! It's a rich man's world!' Money is neither good nor bad but it is necessary. At university money will be an issue: some students have lots, others have none - there is a huge disparity. Whether you will be dependent on student loans, parents or your own earnings, learning how to plan your spending well is essential.

Money is our way of accrediting work. It gives our effort, skill and innovation a value. It's been around in one form or another since people started trading. However, it's also synonymous with power and status, whether it's a multinational buyout, governments exchanging it for resources or the milkman collecting up his dues. Money, as the saying goes, 'makes the world go round.'

Almost 25% of everything Jesus taught in His Sermon on the Mount had something to do with money and possessions. It is a priority subject. Learning how to deal with money effectively is a vital life skill: for now, for university and post education. Most people have an idea of what kind of lifestyle they'd like to have and certain things they'd like to do. Quite often people will talk about being comfortable or having enough. However, this is a little ambiguous because what is enough?

Tent

Spend a few minutes thinking about your money and possessions. Outline your current standard of living (i.e. your own bedroom, food you eat, clothes, possessions, gadgets and toys, leisure and social activities)

_____

_____

_____

How would you sum up your attitude towards money in one sentence?

_____

_____

Mountain

'It is preoccupation with possessions, more than anything else that prevents us from living freely and nobly'

(Thoreau)

Materialism is the governing philosophy of our society. Expressions such as 'He who dies with the most toys wins' underpin a belief in individualistic gain. It feeds our desire to possess more and more things. The West is home to, and the greatest exporter of, materialism; we've built some of the biggest altars. After World War 2 there were just eight shopping malls in the US and now there are nearly 50,000. Shopping is considered to be a holistic experience, a way of life and a leisure activity.

The credit advice bureau reports that on average we have a tendency to spend 10% more than our monthly incomes. It is unsurprising that over six million families in the UK report problems repaying creditors.

Christians are called to be in the culture but not of it. For Western Christians the challenge of stewarding money and resources must be taken seriously and our frame of reference must be the world's poor rather than keeping pace with our Western neighbour.

Craig Bloomberg laments,

> *'Many perceptive observers have sensed that the greatest danger to Western Christianity is not, as is sometimes alleged, prevailing ideologies such as Marxism, Islam, the New Age movement or Humanism but rather the all-pervasive materialism of our affluent culture.'*

Take a look through your last monthly statement on your current account? Where have you spent your money?

_____

_____

_____

If you were to give someone your bank statement, what would it tell them about your beliefs?

Travelling Companion

Nehemiah is someone we can trust to teach us about stewardship and reliance on God. He knows that ultimately everything he has is to be used for the glory of God.

Lakes

Read Nehemiah 1

Nehemiah is moved to compassion to rebuild the walls of Jerusalem. However, his hands are tied. He's in the service of an all-powerful king who could curb such an insolent notion instantly. So Nehemiah prays in which he apologises for his sins and those of his countrymen. He gets right with God.

Nehemiah then trusts God for the opportunity. When it comes he sends an arrow prayer up, via the lump in his throat, and makes his request to the king. He is reliant on God first and he finds favour with the king. God is immensely practical and interested in our physical needs. Nehemiah needed resources and his first port of call was to talk to God.

Campfire

Discuss together:

Do you include God in your practical decisions, for example, which car to buy, which university to go to, how to handle your finances etc?

Share your experiences for decisions you have made.

Lakes

Read Chapter 2:11-19

Nehemiah doesn't rush in and start laying bricks or gathering men. This is a big project and requires forethought and planning. Having sought God, Nehemiah uses his own God-given administration skills; he researches, asks the hard questions and faces the facts.

The job is not an easy one and it quickly becomes apparent he will face resistance. He is rigorous in his preparation. In chapter 3 we see he backs this up with hard work – he doesn't wait for God to do it or make his life easy. Nehemiah's own commitment to seeing his dream out is integral to the process.

> *'But seek first the kingdom of God and all these things will be added to you also.'*

(Matthew 6:33)

Campfire

In light of the first part of the verse above, how would you interpret, 'And all these things will be added to you also'?

Lakes

Read Nehemiah 5:14-19

Nehemiah was proven to be a consistently good steward over 12 years. The reason for this was that he possessed a healthy fear of God. List five good characteristics or actions Nehemiah takes that show him to be a good steward of the resources put in his care.

1._____

2._____

3._____

4._____

5._____

Affluence

God doesn't have a problem with Christians being wealthy, but He does want them to be wealthy and responsible. A redefinition of a millionaire could be someone who gives a million pounds away! We want Christians to be positively influencing the powerful companies in our society. Today's students are tomorrow's leaders in business, education, media and politics.

An inspirational example of a person who handled their money selflessly is John Laing. Laing went into the construction industry and built a multi-million pound business up through his lifetime. When he died, they found John Laing had just £800 cash in his bank account; he'd given it all away.

The Wesley Principle

John Wesley began to limit his expenses so that he would have more money to give to the poor. He records that one year his income was £30 and his living expenses £28, so he had £2 to give away. The next year his income doubled, but he still managed to live on £28, so he had £32 to give to the poor. In the third year, his income jumped to £90. Instead of letting his expenses rise with his income, he kept them to £28 and gave away £62. In the fourth year, he received £120. As before, his expenses were £28, so his giving rose to £92.

One year his income was a little over £1400 pounds. He lived on £30 and gave away the rest. Because he had no family to care for, he had no need for savings. He was afraid of laying up treasures on earth, so the money went out in charity as quickly as it came in. He reports that he never had over £100 at any one time.

Given the challenges raised by our consumer society Richard Foster offers some helpful principles, which offer a helpful safeguard against falling into a consumer mindset if implemented.

*   Buy things for their usefulness rather than their status
*   Develop the habit of giving things away
*   Look with healthy scepticism at all 'buy now pay later' schemes.

Compass

What can you learn from John Laing and John Wesley about God's priorities?

How much do you identify with the three statements above?

Financial Awareness

John Laing and John Wesley came from humble backgrounds and understood the value of things. Whatever our background we must learn and maintain a mindset that never loses sight of the value of things around us. Remember, a bargain is never as cheap as buying nothing at all! We need to know how much change we're due from our tenner - it's just good stewardship.

Test yourself on how much you think the following costs:

An apple _____

A can of coke _____

A litre of petrol _____

A pint of milk _____

1kg of washing powder _____

A light bulb _____

Campfire

How much would you regard reasonable to spend on:

A pair of jeans	_____
A pair of shoes	_____
A mobile phone	_____
A night out	_____
A holiday away with friends	_____
Supporting student mission	_____

Discuss why you would be willing to spend that money.

Rope

Budgeting

A budget is a great way of stewarding our money around our needs. Remember, there may be some hidden cost you've not encountered before so budget for emergencies and the miscellaneous. Be flexible with your budget early on and review it after a term. If you find you fritter money away then a good way of examining the problem is to keep all your receipts in a box and review your spending at the end of each month.

> What is God saying to you?
>
> **Wisdom Box**

Prayer

Dear God you own all the money! Help me to gain an eternal perspective as I seek your kingdom. I pray for wisdom when handling possessions and money so that I might be a good steward. I ask that through your grace I'd apply myself to the discipline of giving so I may be a person who reflects your generosity. Amen.

Landscape: Identity

It's a conditional offer…

In our society acceptance is always conditional. Your worth is measured in success. This is particularly relevant now with your exam results. You have most likely received a conditional offer for your university of choice. With the results either coming out imminently or already known, you're probably now experiencing great pleasure, relief or disappointment. While it is only natural to feel happy or disappointed in the aftermath of results it is important we don't get sucked into connecting the results with our self-worth. If we do, we are missing the deeper reality of who we are in God.

Who are you?

There was a philosopher in Germany named Arthur Schopenhauer. He was a gloomy, melancholic kind of guy who, like a lot of philosophers, would wander down the street with chalk dust on his suit, totally absorbed in some philosophical problem. One day Schopenhauer was walking down the street oblivious to the world around him when he bumped into another man. The man angrily shoved Arthur Schopenhauer and screamed at him, 'Who do you think you are?'

Schopenhauer took that to be a philosophical question. He stopped and stared at the man and said 'Who do I think I am? I only wish I knew. I wish I knew who I was.' He wandered off down the street and was plunged into a major depression as he wrestled with the man's question – 'Who do you think you are?'

Now, very few of us are as obsessive and as focused as someone like Arthur Schopenhauer. And yet the question is there hanging in the air for every one of us – who am I?

Who do you think you are? It is one of the most fundamental questions that you can ask and answer. Who are you really?

Try and write a single sentence below that describes who you are:

_____

_____

Travelling companions

Jesus will be here in thirty minutes. That's the news Martha and Mary heard and it is from these two that we are going to learn more about our identity. Mary and Martha are the most familiar set of sisters in the Bible. Both Luke and John describe them as friends of Jesus. Luke's story, though only four verses long, has been a complex source of inspiration, interpretation, and debate for centuries. You've got thirty minutes until God walks through the door? What are you going to do?

Lakes

Read Luke 10:38-42 and John 12:1-3

> *'What first comes into our minds when we think of God is the most important thing about us'*

(A.W. Tozer)

Tent

Write down in the box below what comes to mind when you think of God.

Wisdom Box

Two responses.

Martha goes into overdrive. 'Oh my goodness!' she cries, 'The house is untidy and guests will need something to eat!' She rushes around and worries about the dinner. Mary smiles, she wanders up to the bathroom and takes out the bottle of perfume she received for her 18th birthday, then camps down beside Jesus.

Campfire

Who is happy on the inside on hearing the news Jesus is coming for tea? Who is worried? Why?

The responses of Mary and Martha underline the two ways the Christian life can be led. One is from a place of acceptance where we live with the inner knowledge that our sins are forgiven and we're free to serve the king. The other is to live in a state of striving, where we consciously, or otherwise, try to work our way into God's favour.

Mark a cross on the continuum below for how you respond to God. Explain why you chose that position.

ACCEPTANCE  STRIVING

Discuss which areas in life you are more prone to striving in. Can you identify why that is the case?

The freed slave

A story is told of an incident that occurred in America before they abolished slavery. Abraham Lincoln bought a slave girl with the sole intention of setting her free. She had no idea what was going on, assuming it was a normal sale. The girl prepared herself for service under her new master. However, once Lincoln had paid the price for her, he gave her the legal documents that told her she was now free.

At first she couldn't understand what was going on. Lincoln had to keep repeating to her 'You're free, you're free!' As the full realisation of what had happened began to sink in, she asked Lincoln, 'Am I free to go wherever I want and do whatever I want to do?'

He replied, 'Indeed you can.'

Then, she said, I choose to stay with you and to serve you gladly for the rest of my days.

'For we did not receive a spirit that makes us a slave again to fear but we received the spirit of sonship and by him we cry, "Abba father". The spirit himself testifies with our spirit that we are God's children.'

(Romans 8:15-16)

The difference between Mary and Martha is that Mary has learned to be accepted in the Father's love. She has learned to soak up the truth of who Jesus is and what He thinks of her.

Mountains

When we've messed up.

We all do: sometimes in a big way, sometimes just without thinking and sometimes just out of our own insecurity and search for identity. Martha complained to Jesus about her sister's lack of help and received a gentle rebuke from Jesus. The disciple Peter went much further and publicly denied Jesus. Jesus takes the initiative in John 21 to restore the relationship and reaffirm he is accepted, loved and trusted.

How do you see yourself when you mess up?

_____

How do you respond to God and others?

_____

Streams

Mary is interested in one thing – being a disciple. Her response to Jesus' arrival is an extravagant sacrificial gift. In pouring out the perfume, she poured her life out before Christ. In the presence of Jesus, Mary understands who she is and can relax with herself and others.

Having discussed acceptance and, in particular, the fact that God still accepts us even when we mess up, take some time to pray that the reality of God's acceptance for you will be understood and felt in your life. Pray specifically into any areas where you have felt shame or where you don't know God's forgiveness and restoration.

Tent

Spend sometime reading over the quote below and then write in the box in your own words who God is to you.

> *'My Father is a watching, running, weeping, laughing, embracing, kissing God. He is an encouraging, affirming, praising, affectionate kind of God. He is a God who loves me so much he cannot keep from embracing me. I am the apple of his eye. He is a God who loves my friendship and just wants me to be with him. A God who enjoys my company even in my failure and my mistakes, because he sees the sincere intentions of my heart. A God who I don't have to strive to make happy, because he has always been happy from the second I turned to him. He is a father who is always cheering me on from the sidelines. He enthusiastically calls me his son.'*

(Mike Bickle)

What is God saying to you?

Wisdom Box

Church in the house

Mary and Martha welcomed Jesus and others into their house. Church took place in the home and was about right relationships with God and other believers. Mary and Martha modelled a dependence on others for their spiritual growth and prioritised and made sacrifices so the 'church' could meet.

Campfire

What role has being part of the church played in your spiritual journey so far?

Do you see your identity as both individual and corporate? Explain why?

How do you feel about joining a new church community if your university is away from home?

Rope

Church connections

Finding a local church at university is the most important thing you can do. Church is not a Christian club, it is a part of your identity that you are called to prioritise and make sacrifices for.

It is worth doing some research and even visiting some churches in your place of study before you start university. A comprehensive list of churches and what they provide for students can be found at **WWW.FUSION.UK.COM.**

Look out for this logo to be linked to churches and other Christians Freshers starting at your university.

What is God saying to you?

Wisdom Box

Prayer

Lord God, I thank you for loving me and accepting me first. Help me become more secure in who I am in you so that being your child is my primary source of identity. Prepare me so that in the new landscape of university I stay committed to you and to your church. Amen.

Landscape: Boldness

'If the Creator had a purpose in equipping us with a neck, he surely meant us to stick it out.'

(Arthur Koestler)

More?

Please Sir, more?' – Oliver Twist's immortal request provokes feelings of excitement, fear and anticipation. As many sit there, the inner battle still churning away inside, one boy is walking arms outstretched, his porridge bowl at the ready.

Boldness is to understand the risks but to still do it. Being bold is to be aware of the circumstances and yet to hold onto the potential prize. Life in studentscape is a time to grow in our boldness for God.

A bold person may be willing to risk shame or rejection in social situations and willingness to bend the rules of etiquette or politeness. Definitive acts of boldness tend to cause an affront to the average mindset because they step onto the ground where our dreams and fears collide. It's an emotive place. Boldness steps outside of the unwritten rules of what is the norm and challenges the status quo.

When was the last time you experienced an inner battle of 'Can I, should I, why can't I?' What happened?

_____

_____

Larry decides to do something…

Larry Walters is a regular guy; a truck driver from San Pedro. One Saturday he's bored with his usual routine so Larry decides to do something. He drops down his local shopping mall and buys 42 weather balloons which he attaches to his strapped down deck chair in his back yard.

When securely tied into the chair, his air pistol nestled in his lap, Larry cuts the ropes. He rises and keeps rising until he levels out at 16,000 ft. Later, air traffic control starts receiving garbled messages from incredulous pilots along the lines of, 'You're not gonna believe this but there's a guy up here in a deck chair!' His thirst for adventure quenched, Larry begins his decent, popping off balloons with his pistol. He lands in Long Beach some seven miles from where he took off.

There is a difference between the boldness needed for thrill seeking and the boldness needed for living for God and representing Him. Naturally timid people who are filled with the Spirit of God can do much greater feats than Larry Walters.

Mountains

Jesus' words were clear as He sent the disciples out: 'Look, I am sending you out as a sheep amongst wolves. Be as wary as snakes and as harmless as doves' (Matthew 10:16). In short, be shrewd and stay innocent. University is a great place, full of opportunities, and where the studentscape culture of autonomy and hedonism is a well-established one.

Making a stand

Many Christians starting a course will wonder how their faith is compatible with university culture. There will be times when it won't be, but then there is a whole new perspective awaiting you.... You're to be an outpost of heaven for those who need to know that God really loves them. That means being in the culture but not of it. You may dress like a student and talk like a student but your primary identity is that of a child of God.

The initial hurdle is to identify yourself with Christ. There is no such thing as a closet Christian. Either, 'The silence kills the Christian or the Christian kills the silence.' This means we need to step out. The good news is that by the time people get to university they are much more respecting and accepting of other people's beliefs and lifestyles. Our role is to continue to break down the stereotypes of Christians being dour, constipated and judgemental and show people how loving, gracious and fun-loving God really is.

Campfire

Discuss together how you are going to make a stand for Christ over the first few crazy weeks at University. It is very probable that your actions will speak much louder than words as you get stuck in and have dirty hands but a clean heart. Write down what that stand could look like.

Wisdom Box

Visit www.loveyouruni.org for more inspiration.

Travelling Companions

Our final companions for the walk up to the university gates are Joshua and Caleb. They are part of the 12-man team sent by Moses to spy out the Promised Land.

Lakes

Read Numbers 13:17-33

What are the biggest challenges/fears you're personally facing with regards to living life for God through university?

List your top three giants:

1. _____

2. _____

3. _____ .

You see giants, I see promises

Caleb and Joshua saw the same land that the others saw. They also saw the same large fortified cities and the same giants strutting around that land. But they measured the situation differently to their fellow spies. They measured by God's promise and not the giants! Often the perspective we hold on to is what makes the difference in how we handle challenges, be they relational or tasks.

Compass

The art of measurement

As you prepare for studentscape and enter into the new landscape of university you can take comfort from knowing that God is with you. However, you will still need to measure and assess the new culture – its mountains and possibilities. Write down below the potential positive possibilities that university could bring and also write down the problems, fears or distractions that may deter you from becoming all God wants you to be.

Possibilities	Mountains

Lakes

Read Joshua 1:1-9

The charge

We all want to know God is with us. Joshua's time had come. He had a big mandate and no doubt felt inadequate. He'd been Moses' assistant – the man who'd led the Israelites out of Israel and for 40 years through the wilderness. Moses had seen God face to face – those were some big shoes to step into! Joshua needed to know God was with him.

> *'This is my command you – be strong and courageous! Do not be afraid or discouraged. For the Lord your God is with you wherever you go.'*

(Joshua 1:9 NLT)

Tent

In these short nine verses Joshua receives at least nine promises from God to deepen his trust in Him so that when Joshua goes into battle he sees the promise and not the giants.

Spend sometime meditating on these verses. What battles does God want to strengthen and prepare you for as you enter university? Which promises do you need to hold onto and make your own?

Wisdom Box

Bold on the inside

Joshua was a breakthrough leader. Breakthrough people exist because there are barriers that need breaking through and there are barriers of unbelief and injustice all around us. We find Joshua as a man standing on the brink. He needs to get this right and hear God. He goes into his tent and spends time alone. When he comes out he knows he has been charged with being bold and courageous. Yes, he's got mates like Caleb hanging around but essentially he's done his business with God and been strengthened on the inside.

WANTED

Students to love their uni

Students who are missional, biblical, relational, catalytic and inclusive

Students who will live beyond themselves, in the culture, with clean hearts and dirty hands

Students who will give beyond themselves, building community and organising parties

Students who will love beyond themselves, dealing grace to broken lives and lonely hearts

FOR CHRIST'S SAKE, WILL YOU LOVEYOURUNI?

Campfire

Discuss together how you can respond to this summons. Where might you need more boldness?

Streams

Pray with someone about the things that this chapter has provoked and ask for God to help you fight the giants and climb the mountains that you face.

Prayer

Lord God, I feel excited/apprehensive/mixed about the three to five years I'm to be at University. I'm aware this will be a time like no other and so want to commit the whole of my student years to you now. Thank you that you are with me and help me live for you and encourage others to live for you. Empower me to be a breakthrough man/woman of God and fill me with your Holy Spirit that I may be bold in representing you. Amen.

studentlinkup.org

360°preparation for uni from [fusion]

Prepare for uni life, find a church,
connect with freshers, keep growing with God,
share your faith, arrive confident and equipped.

"73% of Christian Students don't connect with a church at uni – don't let that be you"

Fusion works with the local church to help freshers find new churches at university.

We help churches welcome new students, develop student workers, disciple their students and get involved in student mission.

If you're a fresher or a student:
- Visit studentlinkup.org to linkup, and find a church.

If you're a youth worker, parent, or know someone starting university:
- Encourage freshers to linkup! You can access help, advice and resources to prepare them for the university experience at studentlinkup.org

Connecting Church to Student
and Student to Church.

Linkup now at
studentlinkup.org

studentlinkup.org
360°preparation for uni from [fusion]
Linkup now!

About : Fusion

The ministry of Fusion emerged in 1997 as a response to a shared vision across the body of Christ to address the challenges of a changing student world. We believe God's passion is for a dynamic student movement, one that will see universities and colleges won for Christ.

Future dreams:

We are about connecting student to church and church to student. Not just one or two but serving thousands of churches in reaching and discipling millions of students. We are convinced that local church needs to be at the heart of student mission and students at the heart of local church.

What we're doing today:

Fusion is fuelling the fires of a national student movement through our three purposes:

EQUIPPING STUDENTS:
Inspiring evangelism, resourcing discipleship and preparing new students for university

SERVING CHURCHES:
Connecting students to church, catalysing mission and strengthening church-based student work

DEVELOPING STUDENT WORKERS:
Training, resourcing and encouraging all those in student ministry

How are we doing it?

Fusion's values under pin all that we do and outline how the mission of Fusion is outworked. We are committed to being:

BIBLICAL, RELATIONAL, MISSIONAL, CATALYTIC AND INCLUSIVE.

Fusion works in partnership at all levels of our organisation. At present we serve in conjunction with around 30 organisations, denominations and church streams. We look to be inclusive and labour alongside those who wish to see a significant move of God in the universities of the UK.

We invite you to partner with us in bringing God's love to the universities, to see a generation respond to Jesus.

Other resources available from Fusion include:

STUDENTSCAPE - A discipleship resource for new students.

THE STUDENT ALPHABET – An A-Z of starting Uni.

THE STUDENT LINKUP TRAINER PACK: Everything you need to prepare school leavers for uni.

THE STUDENT LINKUP STARTING UNI PACK: The must have resource for every school leaver.

UNIVERSITY: THE BIG CHALLENGE - 360° Preparation for student life

WWW.STUDENTLINKUP.ORG - Find and connect to a new church at uni.

FUSE MAGAZINE: News, stories and updates from students and local churches around the country and a directory of churches that welcome and support students.

To find out more please visit *www.fusion.uk.com/resources*

For more information on our resources and the work of Fusion contact us at:

Fusion UK

Unit 18
The Office Village
North Road
Loughborough
LE11 1QJ

☎ 01509 268 505   ✉ hello@fusion.uk.com

www.fusion.uk.com Iwww.studentlinkup.org I www.loveyouruni.org

Notes

Notes

Notes